WRITE THIS WAY

WRITING INTRIGUING INFORMATIONAL PIECES

DiPietro Library
Franklin Pierce University
Rindge, NH 03461

SUE VANDER HOOK

LERNER PUBLICATIONS ◆ MINNEAPOLIS

Lerner Publications Company
A division of Lerner Publishing Group, Inc.
241 First Avenue North
Minneapolis, MN 55401 USA

For reading levels and more information, look up this title at www.lernerbooks.com.

Main body text set in Dante MT Std 12/15. Typeface provided by Monotype.

Library of Congress Cataloging-in-Publication Data

Vander Hook, Sue, 1949–
    Writing intriguing informational pieces / by Sue Vander Hook.
      pages cm. — (Write this way)
    ISBN 978-1-4677-7907-4 (lb : alk. paper) — ISBN 978-1-4677-8284-5 (pb : alk.
paper) — ISBN 978-1-4677-8285-2 (eb pdf)
    1. Exposition (Rhetoric)—Juvenile literature. 2. English language—Rhetoric—
Juvenile literature. 3. Report writing—Juvenile literature. I. Title.
   PE1429.V36 2015
   808'.042—dc23   2015000422

Manufactured in the United States of America
1 – VP – 7/15/15

Table of Contents

Introduction . . . 4

Chapter 1
Pick a Topic . . . 6

Chapter 2
Research Your Topic . . . 12

Chapter 3
Chart Your Writing Course . . . 24

Chapter 4
Write Something—Anything! . . . 28

Chapter 5
Review, Revise, Refine, Rejoice . . . 40

Writing for a Living . . . 46

Source Notes . . . 48

Glossary . . . 50

Selected Bibliography . . . 51

Further Information . . . 52

Index . . . 54

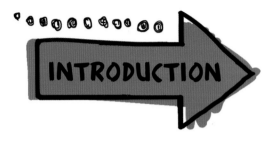

INTRODUCTION

Are you a curious type who loves learning new things? Perhaps animals, nature, or scientific processes fascinate you. Or maybe you're curious about people or places, past or present. If any of these things is true for you, then writing informational pieces may be a great fit for you.

You can find informational writing in magazines and on websites. Entire books can be informational pieces too. **Informational works are different from factual narratives, biographies, and other types of nonfiction. They often tell about things from the natural or social world**—the life cycle of a butterfly, for instance, or the Plymouth Colony, which the pilgrims settled in 1620 after landing at Plymouth Rock. The best informational pieces tell about such things in a clear and concise yet dynamic way. They paint a picture of the facts so vividly that the information stays with you forever.

Think about some real-life facts—an event in nature, a happening in history, or a fascinating creature you'd love to know more about. You can craft those facts into a piece of informational writing that's more than informative—it could be intriguing or even downright thrilling. The best informative writing is like that. It glues readers to their seats just as they would be when reading a gripping mystery novel or adventure story.

Whether you're an eager writer, you insist you can't write, or you're somewhere in between, this book can help you craft informational pieces that no reader will want to put down. It will help you learn how to become a mini expert in your field or subject through in-depth research. It will explain how to hunt for details and find facts beyond what the ordinary person likely knows. From there, you'll learn to write in your own style, using solid writing techniques. Your reward will be an informational piece worthy of pride.

Informational writing is an exciting mission. You can turn your readers into fans of your favorite facts. Writers who can do this are in excellent company. Author and journalist Susan Orlean is one writer who specializes in top-notch informational pieces. Her book *The Orchid Thief: A True Story of Beauty and Obsession* centers on the flower, its history, and people who grow it and collect it, including John Laroche, an obsessed collector who was arrested and fined for stealing wild orchids from a protected area in Florida. Fellow author James W. Hall called the book "the finest piece of nonfiction I've read in years." He said it contains "characters so juicy and wonderfully weird they might have stepped out of a novel, except these people are real." If you aspire to write similarly intriguing informational pieces someday, keep reading. Your readers will be grateful for the time you spent honing your technique and putting your fabulous writing down on paper!

DISCOVER WHAT INTERESTS YOU

OK, you may be thinking, *I thought about what speaks to me. But I still don't know what to write about! How can I choose a topic when there are such a huge number of choices?*

Picking a topic can be overwhelming. Just know that your subject doesn't have to be complicated or unusual. You can begin with a general category or something simple. Here are some questions to get you started:

- What do I like to do?
- What kinds of books do I like to read?
- What interests me when I look out the window?
- What's the most interesting thing going on in the world today?
- Where would I most like to go?
- What's my favorite animal?
- What's fascinating about space?
- What questions do I have about the ocean?
- If I could visit anywhere, where would I go?

Write your answers on a sheet of paper. Don't stop with answering the questions. Keep writing until the sheet is full of words and topics that interest you. If you're having a hard time filling up the paper, ask a friend or family member to write down their answers to some of the questions or some subjects they'd like to know more about.

Perhaps you're thinking the topics on your list are average, maybe even boring. Or perhaps you're wondering how a simple list will help you choose a good topic. Rest assured that a list really *can* be helpful, even if the items on it strike you as pretty commonplace. Ray Bradbury, the famous science fiction writer, was a big fan of lists. He believed that making lists stimulated his creativity and sparked great writing ideas. He wrote, "Lists were the [inspiration], finally, that caused my better stuff to surface." He added, "I was beginning to see a pattern in the list, in these words that I had simply flung forth on paper, trusting my subconscious to give bread, as it were, to the birds." So feed your creativity with a list or two, and then let your lists bring some good "stuff" to the surface.

Look at the words on your lists. Does one of them in particular catch your eye or spark your curiosity? If so, that would be a great thing to write about.

Here's another idea about how to use your lists. Get a pair of scissors and a bowl, a bag, or a box. Cut up your list, separating the words. Put the pieces of paper in the container you chose and mix them up. Next, close your eyes and pick out one piece of paper. This can be your subject! If you're not sure you like the topic, you can pick another one.

TURN THE ORDINARY INTO THE EXTRAORDINARY

Suppose you chose an everyday topic—one that most people probably already know about. That's OK! You can turn the ordinary into the extraordinary. For example, your topic might be fish, which, at first glance, may seem rather blah. Instead of choosing another topic, consider turning that subject into something really interesting. Don't limit yourself to facts about fish in general or to common fish. Find fascinating fish and fish facts to write about. Maybe you can write about a fish that's rare.

Next, visit a library and check out a few books about fish or about the ocean, where some interesting fish live. Flip through the pages until you find some unusual pictures or facts. Make a list of a few facts you didn't know before looking through the books.

You can also go on the Internet and type keywords into a search engine such as Google, Bing, or Yahoo Search. Changing a

Visit a library or search keywords online to help narrow down your topic. Looking through books can help you find interesting facts to write about.

keyword to a similar term can give you more or different results. If you want possible other keywords, look at a thesaurus. Let's say you first searched for "extraordinary fish." You could change "extraordinary" to "unusual," "unique," or "weird."

As you enter keywords, the search engine will produce a list of articles about extraordinary, unusual, or weird fish. It also might produce some pictures of unusual-looking fish, such as the four-eyed spook fish. You might find the Notothenioids, a group of fish species that lives in the frigid waters of the Southern Ocean, which encircles Antarctica. They're interesting because they produce their own antifreeze. It keeps them from freezing in the extremely frigid water. One of these fish could be the one you'll enjoy writing about.

Now you're on your way to creating an informational piece. You've selected a topic and are ready to move on to the next step. Get ready to research!

CHAPTER 2

RESEARCH YOUR TOPIC

Once you decide on a topic, you'll need to ask questions to get information about that topic. Your questions will help you guide your research—or at least get you started.

What questions should you ask? Whatever comes to mind when you think of your topic. Take the example of the Notothenioids. Here are some questions, organized in a table, that you might ask about this unusual type of fish. Use this sample to come up with your own table. Or come up with another creative way to organize your questions and, later, your answers.

Questions	Answers
What is extraordinary about the Notothenioids?	
Where were the fish discovered?	
Why do the fish need to produce the substance that's like antifreeze?	
How did Notothenioid fish start producing antifreeze? How does it work?	

EXPLORE SOURCES

Researching your topic might sound like a less-than-exciting task, or maybe even a daunting one, but it could actually be the most enjoyable part of your informational writing project! Think of it as a mission or a treasure hunt. Don't stop until you find something valuable that makes you say, "wow."

A great place to start your research is your school library or a public library in your community. Library computer systems help you search for just the right books and magazine articles. And once you find something you want to read, you can check it out, take it home, and really dig into the facts it presents. Encyclopedias and textbooks are also good sources for definitions of words and terms you plan to use.

You'll need several descriptive keywords about your subject to put into the library system's search bar. The books or articles you choose can be about specific aspects of your topic, or they can provide general background information. For example, if your topic is electric cars, you might want some specific information about Tesla Motors, an innovative manufacturer of electric cars, and the company's latest ideas for electric vehicles. Tesla makes high-end cars, so you would want to consider including a company or two that manufactures electric cars that are more affordable than what Tesla offers. You could then explain how the cars are different—that is, help readers understand what about the cars results in their different price points. Some general information about the first electric car, built in the mid-1800s, might also be helpful. Facts about the culture and history of that period might make your informative piece even more meaningful.

As you research your topic, write down the titles, authors, and locations of the books you've chosen. Then find them and check them out. Once you have the books, you can set them aside and start your Internet search.

LEARN FROM THE MASTERS

Informational writer Seymour Simon has won many awards for his books about science. Simon was raised in New York City, where he became interested in the insects—and even the weeds—that grew in vacant lots or in the cracks of old buildings he saw. In his nonfiction book *Science in a Vacant Lot*, Simon wrote about the interesting things he found near his home. He discovered that some little creatures can be kept in a jar and later wrote *Pets in a Jar*.

Simon's research style is a little different from that of most other writers. He usually finds photographs first. He researches photos online or takes his own. Next, he puts them in the order he wants them to appear in his book and lays them out on the pages. Finally, he starts writing words that match the photos on the page.

Seymour Simon published *Spiders* in 2007.

When you conduct Internet research, use keywords. To generate keywords, look at some of the books you found or an encyclopedia. What words or ideas stand out for your topic? Keep an eye out for names, places, and dates, which could become important components of your informational piece.

When searching, you may need to get specific to find what you want. When writing about the American Civil War (1861–1865), you may have to specify "American" to avoid getting information about civil wars in other countries. And searching for "Lincoln" may return results for the make of American car by that name and the city in Nebraska, as well as for the president of the United States in office during the Civil War.

When you get a list of results, watch out for websites paid for by advertisers. They often show up at the top of the results page with a special symbol next to them. On Google the symbol is a yellow square with the word *Ad* in it. Because these sites are trying to sell you something, they might not provide accurate information. Below the advertisers' sites, you'll probably find more information than you need for your topic. That means you may have to refine your search and use more specific keywords.

As you read about your subject, you'll discover words that will lead you to more precise information. If you're researching the life cycle of a butterfly, for instance, the word *chrysalis* might spark your interest and generate deeper research.

Use more than the most popular search engines to search for information on your topic. Go beyond Google, Bing, and Yahoo Search. Metasearch engines such as Blingo, Dogpile, and WebCrawler may produce more results. Metasearch engines use the data from several other search engines to find sources for your search. Through your school, you may also have access to databases such as EBSCO, ProQuest, and JSTOR. Databases can be great sources for information. They include scholarly works, such as journal articles. Although material on the Internet hasn't necessarily been edited or reviewed by an expert, researchers and professors have reviewed database articles. Some databases focus on one area, such as medicine or law.

What about Wikipedia? Many people's first instinct is to check this popular site. After all, Wikipedia seems to have an article for almost every topic you can imagine. It's true that Wikipedia is comprehensive, but it's also a wiki—a website that permits any Internet user to alter, add, or delete content. In other words, anyone can open an article and make changes. Wikipedia does monitor its site to catch pranksters who make irresponsible changes, but the organization can't catch everything. This means inaccurate information is more likely to appear on Wikipedia than on, say, a site from a government agency or a university. But wait! This doesn't mean Wikipedia can't be helpful.

Wikipedia can be a good starting point for information. At the bottom of most articles is a list of references. These are the sources the authors used to gather information for the article. The sources often have links users can click on to go to a source, and that may turn out to be quite valuable, providing facts you'll want to include in your informational writing. You may also come across some good keywords you can use for your searches, as well as up-to-the-minute information. Because Wikipedia can be updated so frequently, you may find details there that aren't in the library books you collected.

ASSESS SOURCES

After you've gathered sources, you'll need to assess them to determine if each source is appropriate and reliable. First, consider when the material was published. If you're writing about technology or medicine, you'll want to find the most current information possible. Next, is the material relevant to your topic? Does it support an idea you want to write about or provide information you think will help you create an interesting piece? Then get a sense of the source's accuracy. Keep an eye out for errors in spelling as well as the information itself. Do the facts provided just not add up? Fourth, does the author seem to be an expert? The more qualified the author is, the more reliable the writing. This shouldn't be an issue for sources found in databases. Finally, what's the purpose of the source? This is when you'll need to separate fact from opinion. Focus on facts.

Web sources require an additional check. When assessing Internet sources, pay attention to the domain, or end part of the URL. It provides helpful information. Common domains include

.com (commercial), .org (organization), .edu (education), .gov (government), and .mil (military). Many .com sites belong to businesses that want to sell you something. Organizations with a certain viewpoint often have .org sites, so you'll want to read the information carefully to see if it is fact or opinion.

Once you decide which sources you want to use, be sure to save your source information. You can do this in different ways. You can print the site pages, save the pages as favorites on your computer, or copy the URLs and paste them into a Word document.

SKIM YOUR SOURCES

By now, you should have a lot of sources and information. You're probably wondering how you'll ever read it all. The good news is you don't have to read every word of every source you've gathered. Instead, skim the basic facts.

Skimming doesn't mean reading fast. It means knowing how to quickly find the major ideas and facts. Books are divided into chapters, and articles are split into sections with headings and subheadings. Let's use a magazine article as an example. Follow these steps to skim an article for key facts:

1. <u>Title:</u> Read the title carefully. This tells you the main point of the article.
2. <u>Introduction:</u> Read the entire introduction. This is normally the first one or two paragraphs of the article. The introduction reveals the author's thesis, or main idea. Highlight or make a note of the thesis.
3. <u>Headings and subheadings:</u> Read all the headings and subheadings (usually in bold). They will give you the basic outline of the entire article.
4. <u>First and last sentences:</u> Read the first and last sentences of each section. The first sentence (usually the topic sentence) tells you what the section is about. The last sentence sums up the section.
5. <u>Conclusion:</u> Read the entire conclusion. This is usually the last one or two paragraphs of the article. The conclusion will tell you how the author evaluates and sums up all the facts and ideas in the article.

ORGANIZE NOTES AND QUOTES

Skimming provides the big picture of your topic and some background. The next step is to find the details you'll need to write a good informational piece, one that's highly informative.

Go back to your sources and decide which sections have details you might want to use. Read those sections entirely, keeping an eye out for important facts.

As you read, take lots of notes. Look for answers to the questions you created. Let's look at the example of the Notothenioids. Now the table includes answers.

Questions	Answers
What is extraordinary about the Notothenioids?	Notothenioids naturally produce a substance that's a lot like the antifreeze used in automobiles.
Where were the fish discovered?	The fish were discovered in the Southern Ocean in Antarctica off the shore of McMurdo Sound, where the United States operates a base for Antarctic expeditions.
Why do the fish need to produce the substance that's like antifreeze?	A strong ocean current on the boundary of the Southern Ocean prevents the warmer waters of other oceans from mixing with the extremely cold water of the Southern Ocean. Ordinary fish will freeze to death in those waters. Notothenioids are the only fish that can survive the frigid waters because they produce a substance like antifreeze.
How did Notothenioid fish start producing antifreeze? How does it work?	The fish started producing antifreeze naturally over a period of time when the waters of the Southern Ocean began getting colder and colder. The fish produce antifreeze in their stomach and pancreas.

The more questions you answer, the more fascinating this topic of Notothenioid fish becomes. But go beyond just answering your questions. Write down everything that seems important. For example, based on the answer to the first question, you might want to find out when scientists discovered the antifreeze-like substance that helps the Notothenioids survive in the frigid waters of Antarctica (the answer is 1968).

Be sure to include the name of the source with each note you make so you can easily cite your facts later. If the source is a book or magazine article, write down the page number of the important information.

In your sources, you may also discover statements that would make good quotes in your writing. Quotes from experts on your topic will add credibility to your writing and help your readers trust what you write. Good quotes also include statements by people who have gone through something related to your topic. If you're writing about cancer, for instance, consider using a quote from someone who has had the disease. Readers relate well to people who have seen or experienced something firsthand. Quotes can also add interest and humor.

Keeping track of your quotes and where you got them is important. As you read, stop whenever you notice a strong statement or interesting observation. Copy the quote word for word. You don't want to make any errors in direct quotes. Write down or type the following information so you can credit the source later: author, title, publication, and date. Depending on the source, include a page number or URL as well.

DIG FOR MORE FACTS

By now, you're getting to know your subject pretty well, and you probably have many pages of notes and quotes. But depth is just as important—if not *more* important—than breadth when it comes to research. To write a piece with depth, you'll have to choose one or two main points from your notes and really dig into them.

How do you decide which points to pursue? Simply think about what stood out to you when you were skimming or taking notes. What parts were most intriguing? When you were researching outer space, for example, were the discussions you read about traveling into space your favorite part? Perfect! Then space travel would be a great thing to dig into further.

Where do you start when it comes to digging in? Well, so far, you've most likely been reading secondary sources, or information authors have written about events that have already happened. These writers get their information from research, just as you do. But there's another type of source, the primary source. Looking into such sources is a fantastic next step.

Primary sources are firsthand accounts by people who were at or took part in an event and then told about it. Sally Ride's book *To Space and Back* is a primary source about space travel. Ride participated in space travel and then wrote a book detailing her experiences. Her book would be a good primary source for you to get your hands on if you were writing about space travel.

Sally Ride participated in two spaceflights in the early 1980s. She wrote about her experience in the book *To Space and Back*.

Here are some examples of secondary and primary sources:

Secondary sources	Primary sources
Magazine articles	Diaries or personal journals
Newspaper articles	Letters
Scholarly journal articles	Interviews
Textbooks	Speeches
Nonfiction books	Government documents
History books	Autobiographies
Biographies	Film footage of real events
Encyclopedias	

Another type of primary source is an interview. You probably won't be able to interview an actual astronaut for that space travel piece. But your discussion of space travel might be enhanced if you talked about the first moon landing—and you know that your grandmother remembers the first moon landing. She's talked about it many times. An interview with your grandmother about her memories of the landing might be just the thing you need to give your piece extra pizzazz. To jump-start your interview, think about what you want to know. Write down a few questions to get the conversation started. Here are some possibilities:

- Where were you when the event happened?
- I know you watched the landing on TV. What did you think as you watched?
- What did you feel?

Be careful to avoid closed-ended questions when possible. These are questions that have just a yes or no answer, such as "Did you think the landing was interesting?" Instead, ask open-ended questions that will draw out details. If you ask a closed-ended question, use it to create an open-ended question:

- Closed-ended question—Did you watch the landing alone?
- Open-ended follow-up question—What was the mood in the room as you and your neighbors watched?

You've been busy gathering all kinds of useful information, consulting both primary and secondary sources. It's time for the next step: organizing. Are you ready to chart your writing course? Of course you are! You're doing great—keep moving!

WRITE IT OUT!

During World War 1 (1914–1918), soldiers sometimes wrote journals to pass time in the trenches. These journals have become great primary sources for people who want to find out about what soldiers experienced in the war. Your mission is to write at least five of your own journal entries over the next five days. Write about what's going on in your daily life, but be sure to give it some pizzazz by using descriptive details and zesty language. An effective journal will allow your readers to experience what's going on in your life and share your emotions.

CHAPTER 3

CHART YOUR WRITING COURSE

Your knowledge of the topic you've chosen is growing. Congratulate yourself on picking a topic, finding sources (primary and secondary), learning about your topic, digging for details, and taking lots of notes. You might be wondering what to do with all that information to get it in shape for writing your informational piece. The next step is to get organized and create a writing map that will lead you logically from point A to point B, getting you from an introduction to a conclusion that will captivate your reading audience.

WRITERS ON WRITING

"Nonfiction writers have been out collecting material and now they're getting ready to write, and they've got a great mound of stuff on a table. What are they going to do with it? When I was young, I was so bewildered about how to cope with all that material. Leaning on structural planning is what got me out from under a 50-ton rock that was lying on my chest."

—John McPhee, award-winning nonfiction writer

GET ORGANIZED

The best way to organize so many facts and details is to map them out. Some writers like to arrange their information in an outline something like this:

I.   Introduction
    A. An attention-getter with a real-life example
    B. Thesis—the central idea
    C. The path you'll take—a few hints about what's to come: topics 1, 2, and 3
    D. Conclusion/transition
II. Body
    A. Main point 1
        1. Subpoint: supporting information
        2. Subpoint: supporting information
        3. Conclusion/transition
    B. Main point 2
        1. Subpoint: supporting information
        2. Subpoint: supporting information
        3. Conclusion/transition
    C. Main point 3
        1. Subpoint: supporting information
        2. Subpoint: supporting information
        3. Conclusion/transition
III. Conclusion/closing summary
    A. Restate topics
    B. Concluding statement

If you were writing a book about your state, you could start your introduction with an interesting historical fact, or you might set the scene by describing a walk through an area with some well-known attractions. After you set up your thesis and hint at what's to come, you'll write the body of your piece. That would include several main points, such as history, geography and climate, wildlife, economics, and population. The subpoints would be some of the facts you gathered about your state.

Instead of a traditional outline, some writers like to use a writing map, or a graphic organizer. This is a picture of what's stored in your head and in your notes. It will help you see what you're thinking and how your facts relate to one another. Writing maps can take on just about any shape or form. One style uses a main circle that has spokes that connect to smaller circles. The smaller circles may also have spokes that connect to still smaller circles. The largest circle is the topic of your paper. The next level of circles indicates the main points, with one point in each circle, and so on down the line.

If you choose to create a writing map, yours might be a maze of roads that lead to your thesis. Whatever design your map takes, be sure it makes good sense to you so you can easily translate it into words.

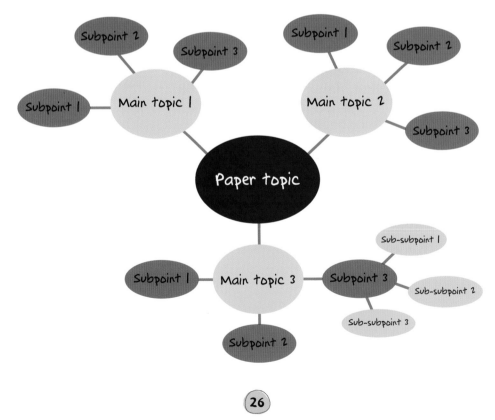

INCLUDE GRAPHICS

While researching your topic, you probably noticed pictures and other images in your sources. Did the visuals make the sources more interesting or help you understand the topic better? Your answer is probably yes. That's why adding images—photos, drawings, maps, and graphs—to your writing can be effective.

Using images has several benefits. A picture, a map, a table, or another visual can help you condense long, wordy explanations. Instead of describing something in several sentences, you can show it in a graphic. Such visual aids can help readers see how your facts fit together or relate to one another. Visual information will stand out on the page and highlight why those facts are significant. If you're writing about how your state has changed in the last ten years, for instance, you might include a table showing the state's population in each of those years.

Once you've looked for or created graphics, you're ready for the next step: writing. You've done a lot of work to get to this point. Your research and organization are about to pay off.

WRITE SOMETHING—ANYTHING!

Does thinking about writing make you freeze in your tracks? Not to worry. Sure, some people dive right into the writing process. But many others feel a little scared by the whole thing. It can seem pretty overwhelming. If you tend to feel scared—or even if you normally dive in but just find yourself feeling stuck—don't get discouraged. You're in really good company.

One of the best solutions to writer's block is to allow yourself to write imperfectly, even badly. People often don't allow themselves to put words on a page because they're afraid the words won't be perfect. They're afraid to write badly, so they don't write anything. Overcoming writer's block means allowing yourself to put words—any words—on the page. Remember, your goal is to start writing. What you put on paper now isn't the final product.

AVOID PLAGIARISM

When writer's block sets in, be careful not to plagiarize. When you can't think of what to write, using someone else's words may be tempting. Copying portions of your research and using them as your own seems easy. Or you might believe changing a few words around and making a sentence that's similar to a

sentence in your research is OK. You might think it's not copying because the sentence is slightly different. It's not OK. Plagiarism is defined as using someone else's words or ideas and passing them off as your own. This means that using even a portion of someone else's words is plagiarism. And any degree of plagiarism is unacceptable.

So put some words—your *own* words—on the page and start your informational piece. Sometimes it helps to talk through the first few sentences. Say something out loud, and then write down those words. Do it quickly, before you forget what you said. And don't worry about how the words sound or whether they are grammatically correct. Just get your ideas on the page and keep going. Once you get started, you may find your mind is flooded with ideas.

DRAFT AN ENGAGING INTRODUCTION

Getting words on the page is a great start. Remember, your piece has to start somewhere.

The introduction sets up the path your piece is going to follow. An introduction is also a way to get readers' attention. If the first few sentences aren't engaging, the reader may very well not read on.

Sylvia A. Earle and Linda K. Glover began the book *Ocean: An Illustrated Atlas* by setting a scene:

> *Cold, bleak, barren, inhospitable to life—that is what Earth would be without the flowing blue mantle that engulfs the planet's highest mountains, rolls over the deepest valleys, sweeps across the broadest plains, and covers most of the planet's surface, with the only substance that living creatures absolutely require— water. Astronauts looking at the blue Earth from afar readily see what most terrestrial primates do not: This planet is dominated by water. . . . Earth is an ocean where even the largest landmasses are islands surrounded by a single, interconnected body of water.*

What an intriguing introduction! But what is it that makes it so interesting? Perhaps it's the descriptive adjectives (bleak, barren, inhospitable) or the feeling that you're soaring over the surface of Earth, swooping over the mountains and diving into the valleys. The authors' carefully chosen words make readers experience Earth, not just read about it.

A good way to learn how to write an interesting introduction is to read the introductions other writers have created for their informational pieces. Read a few magazine or newspaper articles, and then read more.

As you peruse more and more introductions, you'll get a sense of what works well. Pay attention to what grabs you. If it grabs you, the writing is doing what it's supposed to do. You'll also probably start to think of ideas for your own introduction. Maybe you'll go back and review some of the most interesting facts or quotes from your research. Would any of them work as an introduction? Decide how you'll start your piece. Remember, in addition to an attention grabber, your introduction should include a thesis and a hint of what path your informational piece is going to take.

KEEP IT MOVING

Once you write your introduction, move to the body of your text. Don't jump off a cliff as you travel from the introduction to the rest of the text. Use a clear, interesting transition sentence to slide smoothly from one to the other. The sentence will show the logical relationship between the introduction and the first main point.

A mere word or two might trigger a transition. The following table includes some useful transitional words:

To show	In time	In addition	To clarify	To conclude
For example	Afterward	Moreover	In other words	With this in mind
To illustrate	Next	Besides	That is	Finally
Specifically	Then	Further	In fact	In short
Such as	While	Also	More clearly	To sum up
For instance	During	Then again	To put it simply	In the end

Consider an example from Jason Bittel's piece "Four Weird Ways Animals Sense the World." He began the *National Geographic* article with this introduction:

When humans sniff in order to smell something, we draw a quick puff of air into our nostrils and over chemoreceptors in our nasal cavity. But octopuses, butterflies, and other animals don't have noses like ours. Instead, they've evolved other, sometimes bizarre ways of sensing the world around them.

He followed by writing this:

For instance, if you were to look closely at an Oregon shore crab (Hemigrapsus oregonensis)*, you wouldn't see anything resembling a nose. But that doesn't mean the creatures have no sense of smell.*

Bittel moved readers on from his introduction and into the story with a simple "for instance." It built on his introduction by setting up readers for an example of an animal that has developed an alternative to a nose. Be sure to do the same when you write. Use a transition sentence whenever you move from one point to the next. That will keep your text moving smoothly and make your path logical, which will engage and inform readers.

As you write, don't forget the outline or writing map you created to guide your writing. Refer back to it to make sure you're following the well-planned path you worked hard to create.

WRITERS ON WRITING
"I know some very great writers, writers you love who write beautifully and have made a great deal of money, and not one of them sits down routinely feeling wildly enthusiastic and confident. Not one of them writes elegant first drafts. All right, one of them does, but we do not like her very much."

—Anne Lamott, Bird by Bird

Each entry or step is a main point. Pace yourself as you move through those main points. Control your speed as you move through the events and details you want to cover. Keep readers moving so they don't get bored, but be sure to fully develop each of your points. Be sure to use transition sentences throughout your writing to move smoothly from one point to the next. And don't forget to keep it interesting—don't simply list facts.

FIND RELEVANT QUOTES

One way to keep your readers interested in your topic is to intersperse quotes in your writing. Quotes should support or add to the information you're providing. A strong quote from an expert who backs up what you're saying increases your credibility as a writer. It also brings in another voice and tone, which in turn add interest.

When you quote someone, include that person's name, their title, and who they work for. For example, if you quote a scientist, indicate that the person is a scientist and the organization with which he or she is associated.

Imagine you're writing a book about space. Including a quote by Neil deGrasse Tyson would be a great idea. He's an astrophysicist, or space scientist. He's also well known in his field and to the general public. When quoting Tyson, you would note that he's an astrophysicist at the American Museum of Natural History.

It's fairly simple to incorporate a quote into your writing, as long as you're careful to include your source. Here's how writer Burkhard Bilger wrote about some early Mars explorations in a *New Yorker* magazine article:

> *"Given all the evidence presently available, we believe it entirely reasonable that Mars is inhabited with*

living organisms and that life independently originated there," a study by the National Academy of Sciences concluded in March 1965.

In the above example, Bilger's source is the National Academy of Sciences. When you quote someone, let readers know your source. Your readers need to know where the quote came from. You'll also want to identify any ideas you got from someone else. This is called citing your sources, and it adds to your credibility and makes you trustworthy as a writer.

Depending on what you're writing, such as a research paper, you may cite your source after a quote or idea. To do this, provide information in parentheses immediately after the quote or idea. Multiple styles exist for citing sources. Two of the most common are MLA (Modern Language Association) and APA (American Psychological Association). For MLA, you would place the author's name in the parentheses. For APA, you would place the name and the year of publication. Here are examples of both using the previous quotation:

MLA: *" '. . . with living organisms and that life independently originated there,' a study by the National Academy of Sciences concluded in March 1965" (Bilger).*

APA: *" '. . . with living organisms and that life independently originated there,' a study by the National Academy of Sciences concluded in March 1965" (Bilger, 2013).*

Providing material in parentheses is only half of the citation process. You'll also want to provide a full reference on your works cited page, which is a list of all the sources you quote in your text. You'll create that last, after you've drafted a conclusion to your piece.

LEARN FROM THE MASTERS

Rebecca L. Johnson writes about science and nature for younger readers. Johnson's work has taken her to all kinds of places, from mountaintops to the ocean floor. The book *Alice in Wonderland* made her want to become a writer. She wanted to see new places and creatures just as Alice did. Johnson built on her inspiration with her education. She explained:

> Science was the key that opened my doorway to adventure, and to writing. In college, I earned advanced degrees in both biological science and graphic design. I worked for a few years writing college biology textbooks but then started writing nonfiction for kids, mostly books with a nature or environmental focus. I began contacting scientists doing research in these fields and was invited to join all sorts of expeditions, on land and at sea.

Rebecca L. Johnson (above) has published numerous science books for young adults. Her books include *Zombie Makers: True Stories of Nature's Undead* and *When Lunch Fights Back: Wickedly Clever Animal Defenses.*

With inspiration, education, and dedication, Johnson has created a successful, fulfilling career writing informational pieces.

FINISH WITH A PURPOSE

Once you've traveled your path of main points, subpoints, and sub-subpoints, adding quotes along the way, you're ready to end your informational piece. **A conclusion is more than a paragraph to sum up your main points and ideas or repeat your introduction. It's a meaningful paragraph—or two—that allows you to finish with a purpose.**

A conclusion is significant. It lets readers know why all the information that led up to it matters to them or to others. The conclusion is your last chance to prove that what you wrote was well worth reading. Remember the quote from the great introduction Earle and Glover wrote for *Ocean: An Illustrated Atlas*? After providing an abundance of information about the world's oceans and ocean exploration, the authors discussed the ocean's future in the final chapter of the book. Here's how they concluded that chapter:

> *The deep and dark blue ocean will continue to roll—far into the future—but it is increasingly clear that it is unrealistic to take for granted the benefits it provides, the distillation of four and a half billion years of fine-tuning. Never before has there been a greater need to understand all aspects of the deep frontier and to provide a sound knowledge base for crucial decisions that will otherwise be made in ignorance. And never again will there be better opportunities to explore and protect the natural ocean systems that are crucial to the future of humankind on this ocean planet.*

What makes this conclusion good? First, it briefly recaps what led up to it, including the importance of understanding and exploring the world's oceans. Then it ends on a positive note by stating plainly and clearly that action is needed to preserve the world's waters.

You can create an equally powerful conclusion. You may not do it on your first (or second or even third) try. That's what revising is for. But you have one more thing to do before you revise.

CREATE A BIBLIOGRAPHY AND A LIST OF WORKS CITED

Once you've completed your draft, you'll need to write a bibliography. A bibliography is a list of all the sources you used to write your informational piece. It includes books, articles (magazine, newspaper, encyclopedia, database), interviews—whatever you consulted to write your draft. Each entry, called a reference, includes the name of the author(s), the title of the piece, the publisher, and other information, depending on the source. Even if you don't quote the sources, include them in your bibliography because they gave you background information on your topic.

In the academic world, there are two basic styles for citing and formatting sources for an informative piece. The examples below show two samples of the differences in citation styles.

	MLA (Modern Language Association)	APA (American Psychological Association)
Book	Frank, Anne. *Anne Frank: The Diary of a Young Girl.* New York: Bantam, 1993. Print.	Frank, A. (1993). *Anne Frank: The diary of a young girl.* New York: Bantam.
Academic journal	Sidell, B., and O'Brien, K. "When Bad Things Happen to Good Fish: The Loss of Hemoglobin Expression in Antarctic Icefishes." *The Journal of Experimental Biology* 209 (2006): 1791–1802. Print.	Sidell, B., and O'Brien, K. (2006). When bad things happen to good fish: The loss of hemoglobin expression in Antarctic icefishes. *The Journal of Experimental Biology,* 209, 1791–1802.

Next, create a list of works cited. Some people call this list source notes. This list is a variation of your bibliography. It will consist of only those sources you quoted. And for print publications, such as books and magazines, you'll need to add the page number where the quoted material is located. As with your bibliography, you'll need to follow a particular style for your list of works cited.

Once you complete your bibliography and list of works cited, that's it—you did it! You wrote an informational piece. You know, of course, that you aren't done—but you are well on your way. Now that you've created a first draft, it's time to revise. You'll do that next with the help of some thoughtful editing—by yourself and others.

CHAPTER 5

REVIEW, REVISE, REFINE, REJOICE

You're in the homestretch! Before finishing your informational piece, take an inventory of what you've accomplished so far:

1. You found an interesting topic.
2. You researched your topic and learned all kinds of fascinating facts.
3. You dared to write badly and put a lot of the information you gathered in your research on the page in your own words.
4. You discovered a way to make your introduction engaging.
5. You conquered transition sentences.
6. You kept moving through your points, subpoints, and sub-subpoints in an organized, interesting way.
7. You finished with a purpose.
8. You created a bibliography and a list of works cited.

Kudos to you for a lot of hard work! Be proud of what you've done. Next, take a break from your draft. Staying away from your writing for a day or two is often helpful. When you return to your draft, you'll see it from a new perspective. You won't be so immersed in your piece and will be ready to evaluate it, change it, and polish it, adding words and details to make it even stronger, more interesting, and easier to read.

CUT, REWRITE, CUT, AND ADD

Most famous authors admit they change their manuscripts many times. For example, legendary journalist and fiction writer Ernest Hemingway described in an interview a specific experience he had while writing a fictional piece: "I rewrote the ending of *Farewell to Arms*, the last page of it, 39 times before I was satisfied."

Now it's your turn to polish your draft. This means you can cut material, add material—then cut and add again—and change what you wrote initially. If you read something that seems boring, change it or even cut it. Add some descriptive details and adjectives. Change your scenes so readers can see, feel, hear, smell, and taste what you're describing.

When you've revised your draft completely, walk away from it again, for another day or two. When you return to it, reread your informational piece and revise anything you think you can improve. You may find that a revision you made during your first round of changes doesn't sound the same during the second round and you can improve it. Keep revising until it sounds great and is extremely interesting when you read it out loud. When you accomplish that, you'll be ready to clean up the grammar and make your informational piece structurally correct.

POLISH UP THE GRAMMAR

Maybe you're wondering why you have to work on the grammar if your piece is interesting and sounds good. Isn't writing a personal creation, a work of art? Yes and no. Writing is definitely your own creative achievement. But you don't want to risk looking uneducated or unintelligent. If your writing is full of grammatical errors, your readers may not take it seriously. In fact, poor grammar may keep them from reading your entire piece.

Grammatical errors are pretty common. A good writer will do everything possible to fix those mistakes before anyone reads his or her writing. One of the most common grammatical errors is using the wrong form of a word. This list is a good reference for some of the most misused words.

Word	Meaning
there	at or in a certain place
their	belonging to people or things
they're	a contraction for "they are"
two	a number; the sum of one plus one
to	in the direction of
too	also; excessively
your	belonging to a person or people
you're	a contraction for "you are"
its	belonging to a thing
it's	a contraction for "it is"
here	at this place
hear	to sense through the ear
whose	belonging to a certain person
who's	a contraction for "who is"

Punctuation is also important. Commas help readers get the meaning you intended in your writing. A missing or extra comma can sometimes change the meaning of a sentence. Consider the following two sentences:

- Let's eat Grandma.
- Let's eat, Grandma.

Which one communicates the intended meaning? The first sentence might be a line in a zombie movie. It's the second one you want to use, assuming you'd like to sit down to a meal with your grandma.

LEARN FROM THE MASTERS

Alexander Chee (below) is an award-winning fiction author. He writes essays and short stories as well, and he has taught fiction and nonfiction writing. In 2012 he offered five writing tips on the Asian American Writers' Workshop website. Tip 3 was about revising: "When revisions seem impossible, try retyping. Open a blank file, use the printout, and see what happens—usually something better starts to appear. In the age of the computer, we can get so into cutting and pasting, and the truth of a sentence after another sentence is you are making a kind of energetic momentum—cutting and pasting it can kill the sequence, send the charge falling apart. Retyping can put that back together."

Working with commas takes time and practice. Two guidelines to help you start mastering them are to use a comma before the words *and* or *or* in a list of three or more items and after an introductory phrase, such as "Early Saturday morning." Here are some example sentences that follow these rules:

- The US flag is red, white, and blue.
- Early Saturday morning, the cat curled up on my pillow.

English has many rules about both punctuation and grammar. If you conquer this much, you'll be on the road to crafting high-quality writing. If you want to know more about the nuts and bolts of English, Mignon Fogarty's Grammar Girl website (http://www.quickanddirtytips.com/grammar-girl) is one of many helpful sites available to writers. According to Fogarty, the site is "your friendly guide to the world of grammar, punctuation, usage, and fun developments in the English language."

Now that you're armed with this important information about commas and apostrophes, read your informational piece again. This time, do it with an eye for these important details. You can even make this task a search-and-find game by counting the errors you identify and fix.

GET FEEDBACK

Find at least one person to read your piece and provide feedback. Family members, friends, and teachers all make great reviewers. Let that person be totally honest and suggest how you could improve your writing. Ask your reviewer to write down what's great about your piece, what could be better, and what isn't working. Ask your reviewer if he or she found your piece interesting and if any information was new. You could also ask if

Ask a parent or friend to read your informational piece. Do another round of revisions on any section that your reader found confusing.

any questions came up while he or she read. If so, you may want to add information to answer that question. Then it's time for another round of revisions to incorporate your reviewer's suggestions.

There's one more step to this writing process. You need to find someone who's willing to be your editor. That person should be a good writer and know about the rules of grammar. Ask your editor to mark up your piece and write comments in the margins. Then you're ready to make a final pass at your creation to refine this work you've put so much effort into. One last time, search for the best way to say exactly what *you* want to say to make your writing extraordinary.

That's it! You've reached the finish line! You researched your topic and became a mini expert on it. You wrote an engaging introduction, and you made the facts you gathered come to life with great organization and thoughtful, descriptive words. Finally, you ended it with a purpose and gave your readers new information and a new experience. You reviewed, revised, and refined. It's time to rejoice. Way to go!

WRITING FOR A LIVING

Endless possibilities exist for someone who wants to write about remarkable things—animals, people, places, things, weather, scientific processes, the wonders of space or, really, anything in the universe. People who write about fascinating facts are all authors, and they work in a variety of careers.

Some informational authors are independent writers who write books and then submit them to publishers who prepare their manuscripts for printing and publication. Some publishers hire authors to write about an assigned topic, usually as part of a series of books.

Magazines and newspapers rely on quality informational writing. Authors can break into this field by submitting interesting informational articles to magazines or newspapers that might be interested in their topic. For example, a long-distance trail runner who writes about his or her recent race experience might submit an article to a magazine such as *Trail Runner*. Someone who writes about horses could pitch an article to *Horse&Rider*.

Journalism is an option for writers who want to work at a full-time job in informational writing. Some journalists write high-interest articles and sometimes travel to interesting places to do their research. *National Geographic*, *Scientific American*, and *Sports Illustrated* are only a few of the magazines that hire informational writers. A journalist's potential audience comprises the people of the world— anyone who reads or hears what the journalist writes.

Book publishers, magazines, newspapers, and websites are looking for writers who can create great texts about what goes on in the universe. They're looking for people who can make life interesting with words that captivate and engage readers. Nonfiction sells, and people want to read true stories. If you're interested in writing, compile a list of publishers who sell nonfiction books or publish informational articles. Then write a convincing letter to send with your manuscript. Tell the publisher why your book or article is unique and why people will want to read it.

SOURCE NOTES

5   "The Orchid Thief Summary & Study Guide," *BookRags*, accessed February 12, 2015, http://www.bookrags.com/studyguide-the -orchid-thief/#gsc.tab=0

7   "Yale Literary Magazine Interview with Susan Orlean,"*Susan Orlean* (blog), accessed February 12, 2015, http://www .susanorlean.com/news/yaleinterview.html.

8–9   Maria Popova, "Ray Bradbury on How List-Making Can Boost Your Creativity," *Brain Pickings*, accessed February 17, 2005, http://www.brainpickings.org/2013/10/18/ray-bradbury -on-lists/.

17   Gail Gibbons, home page, last modified March 29, 2012, http:// www.gailgibbons.com/.

24   Jennifer Greenstein Altmann, "Assembling the Written Word: McPhee Reveals How the Pieces Go Together," *News at Princeton*, May 7, 2007, http://www.princeton.edu/main/news/archive /S17/83/14G28/index.xml?section=featured.

29   Jeryl Brunner, "Famous Writers Share How They Handle Writer's Block," *Huffington Post*, January 29, 2015, http://www .huffingtonpost.com/jeryl-brunner/famous-writers-share-how -_b_6560188.html.

30   Michael Matz, "Fish: Fresh, Not Frozen," *Origins*, accessed February 17, 2015, http://www.exploratorium.edu/origins /antarctica/ideas/fish.html.

31   Sylvia A. Earle and Linda K. Glover, *Ocean: An Illustrated Atlas* (Washington, DC: National Geographic Society, 2009), 26.

32   Jason Bittel, "Four Weird Ways Animals Sense the World," *National Geographic*, November 22, 2014, accessed February 16, 2015, http://news.nationalgeographic.com/news/2014/11/141122-crabs-snakes-smell-taste-nose-science-biology/.

33   Ibid.

33   Anne Lamott, "Bird by Bird Quotes," *Goodreads*, accessed February 17, 2015, https://www.goodreads.com/work/quotes/841198-bird-by-bird-some-instructions-on-writing-and-life.

34–35   Burkhard Bilger, "The Martian Chroniclers," *New Yorker*, April 22, 2013, http://www.newyorker.com/magazine/2013/04/22/the-martian-chroniclers.

36   Rebecca Johnson, home page, accessed February 16, 2015, http://www.rebeccajohnsonbooks.com/about-rebecca/.

37   Earle and Glover, *Ocean*, 322.

41   Emily Temple, "20 Great Writers on the Art of Revision," *Flavorwire*, January 8, 2013, http://flavorwire.com/361311/20-great-writers-on-the-art-of-revision/view-all.

43   Alexander Chee, "Writing Tips: 'Style without Story Is an Empty Suit,'" *Margins*, November 20, 2012, http://aaww.org/alex-chees-writing-tips-style-without-story-is-an-empty-suit/.

44   Mignon Fogarty, "Grammar Girl," Mignon Fogarty and Macmillan Holdings, accessed February 16, 2015, http://www.quickanddirtytips.com/grammar-girl.

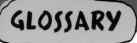

GLOSSARY

bibliography: an alphabetical list of books, articles, and other sources a writer uses for research

editor: someone who makes changes or corrections to something, including someone who works with writing to increase its readability, accuracy, and logic

keyword: a word or phrase that can be used to search for books, websites, or articles

plagiarism: using another person's words or ideas and passing them off as one's own

primary source: a document or item written or created during the time in question

secondary source: a book, article, or other source created based on research of a topic or event

transition sentence: a sentence that smoothly connects one idea to the next and signals the reader that the writer is moving on to the next point

writer's block: the state of being unable or afraid to write

SELECTED BIBLIOGRAPHY

Earle, Sylvia A., and Linda K. Glover. *Ocean: An Illustrated Atlas*. Washington, DC: National Geographic Society, 2009.

Gibbons, Gail. Home page. Last modified March 29, 2012. http://www.gailgibbons.com/.

Lamott, Anne. "Bird by Bird Quotes." *Goodreads*. Accessed on January 27, 2015. https://www.goodreads.com/work/quotes/841198-bird-by-bird-some-instructions-on-writing-and-life.

Matulka, Rebecca. "The History of the Electric Car." September 15, 2014. http://energy.gov/articles/history-electric-car.

Matz, Michael. "Fish: Fresh, Not Frozen." *Origins*. Accessed January 27, 2015. http://www.exploratorium.edu/origins/antarctica/ideas/fish.html.

"Yale Literary Magazine Interview with Susan Orlean." *Susan Orlean* (blog). Accessed January 27, 2015. http://www.susanorlean.com/news/yaleinterview.html.

A+ Research & Writing
http://www.ipl.org/div/aplus
Check out this site for research and writing guidance, including a step-by-step process for researching and writing a paper.

Allen, Moira Anderson. *Starting Your Career as a Freelance Writer.* New York: Allworth, 2011. Allen addresses a variety of topics an aspiring freelancer might encounter, including making time for writing, setting goals, writing for different markets, writing for print and for the web, and dealing with rejection.

Bell, James Scott. *How to Make a Living as a Writer.* Woodland Hills, CA: Compendium, 2014. This book offers more than two dozen chapters of information on becoming a successful professional writer, including self-publishing and traditional publishing, time management, self-editing, and writing in different genres.

Bodden, Valerie. *Write and Revise Your Project.* Minneapolis: Lerner Publications, 2015. Check out this book for guidance on crafting a great research paper or presentation.

Go Teen Writers
http://goteenwriters.blogspot.com
This website offers tips, connections, and encouragement for young writers.

Grammar Rules! New York: Time for Kids, 2013. The editors of Time for Kids compiled this book for young readers who want to learn about English, including parts of speech and punctuation.

Merriam-Webster. *Webster's Thesaurus for Students*. 3rd ed. Springfield, MA: Federal Street, 2010. Use this reference book to add word variety to your writing and to expand your vocabulary.

Reading and Writing for Kids http://kids.usa.gov/teens/reading-and-writing/index.shtml This site by the US government has links to information about important American authors and reading and writing jobs, among other resources.

Schwab, Christine. *Grammar, Grades 7–8*. Greensboro, NC: Carson-Dellosa, 2015. Check out this workbook for information and exercises designed to help you hone your knowledge of English grammar.

Truss, Lynne. *Eats, Shoots & Leaves: The Zero Tolerance Approach to Punctuation*. New York: Gotham, 2003. This book gives helpful, entertaining answers to your punctuation questions.

Vander Hook, Sue. *Writing Notable Narrative Nonfiction*. Minneapolis: Lerner Publications, 2016. This handy writing guide offers practical ideas for writing creative, engaging narrative nonfiction.

INDEX

bibliography, 38–39, 40
Bilger, Burkhard, 34–35
Bittel, Jason, 32–33
Bradbury, Ray, 8–9

citing sources, 20, 35–37
conclusion, 18, 24–25, 37–38

databases, 15–16, 38
drafts, 30, 38–39, 40–41

Earle, Sylvia A., 31, 37

feedback, 44–45

Glover, Linda K., 31, 37
grammar, 41–45

Hemingway, Ernest, 41

interviews, 22–23, 38
introduction, 18, 24–25, 30–33, 37, 40, 45

keywords, 10–11, 13–15, 16

metasearch engines, 15

nonfiction, 4–5, 7, 24, 36

online resources, 9, 13–17
Orlean, Susan, 5, 7
outlines, 25–26, 33

plagiarism, 28–30
primary sources, 21–23, 24
print resources, 13

quotes, 20, 31, 34–35, 37, 39

reliable sources, 16
research, 5, 11, 12–16, 17, 20–21, 27, 28–29, 30, 31, 35, 40, 45
revising, 38–45
Ride, Sally, 21

search engines, 10–11, 15
secondary sources, 21–23, 24

thesis, 18, 25–26, 27, 31
tone, 34
topic, 6–16, 18–20, 24–27, 34, 38, 40, 45
topic sentence, 18
transition sentences, 32–34, 40

visual aids, 27
voice, 34

works cited, 35, 38–39, 40
writer's block, 28–29
writing map, 24, 26, 33

PHOTO ACKNOWLEDGMENTS

The images in this book are used with the permission of: © Eric Isselee/Shutterstock.com, p. 6; © Amanda Edwards/FilmMagic/Getty Images, p. 7; © iStockphoto.com/deepblue4you, p. 9; © Sam Bloomberg-Rissman/Blend Images/Getty Images, p. 10; KRT/Newscom, p. 14; © iStockphoto.com/AlesVeluscek, p. 17; NASA, p. 21; © Oscar White/CORBIS, p. 24; © Marks Narodenko/Shutterstock.com, p. 27; © Martin Godwin/Getty Images, p. 29; © Diane Cohen/Demotix/CORBIS, p. 33; © Ann Parks Hawthorne, p. 36; © M. Sharkey, p. 43; © Erin Patrice O'Brien/Getty Images, p. 44; © koosen/Shutterstock.com (cardboard background); © Everything/Shutterstock.com (spiral notebook); © AtthameeNi/Shutterstock.com (grid paper); © oleschwantder/Shutterstock.com (yellow lined paper).

Cover: © koosen/Shutterstock.com (cardboard); © oleschwantder/Shutterstcock.com (yellow lined paper).

ABOUT THE AUTHOR

Sue Vander Hook is the author of more than forty books, including biographies and books on writing, technology, sports, disease, and historical events. "My passion," she says, "is to make the world exciting and interesting to young readers. I enjoy bringing history to life and creating scenes that readers can 'see' and experience. It is my privilege to pass along writing tips to young writers who have a story to tell and need the encouragement to write it down." Vander Hook has a master's degree in English studies from Minnesota State University, Mankato, where she also taught writing.

DATE DUE